Instructions on page 50.

Instructions on page 51.

3

4

Instructions on page 52.

6

Instructions on page 54.

Instructions on page 55.

8

Instructions on page 56.

16

Instructions on page 64.

Instructions on page 65.

18

Instructions on page 66.

LIFE IS SWEET 1987

SAMPLERS

Instructions ·on· page ·68.

Instructions on page 69.

Instructions on pages 70, 71.

23

LANDSCAPE

Instructions on page 74.

Instructions on page 75.

28

Instructions on page 76.

Instructions on page 77.

Motifs for Children

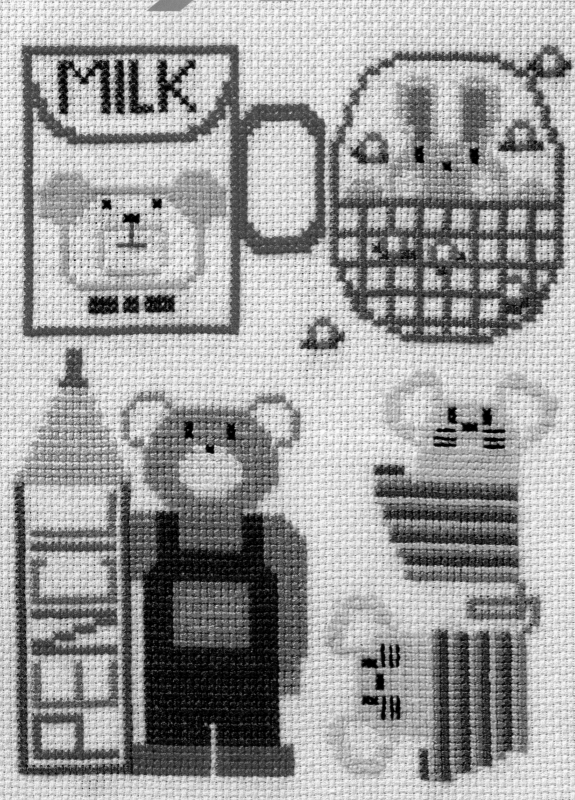

Instructions on page 78.

Instructions on page 80.

34

Instructions on page 82.

36   Instructions on page 84.

Instructions on page 85.

Alphabets, Geometric and Repeating Designs

Instructions on page 86.

Instructions on page 87.

Instructions on page 88.

Instructions on page 89.

41.

42   Instructions on page 90.

Instructions on page 91.

44

Instructions on page 92.

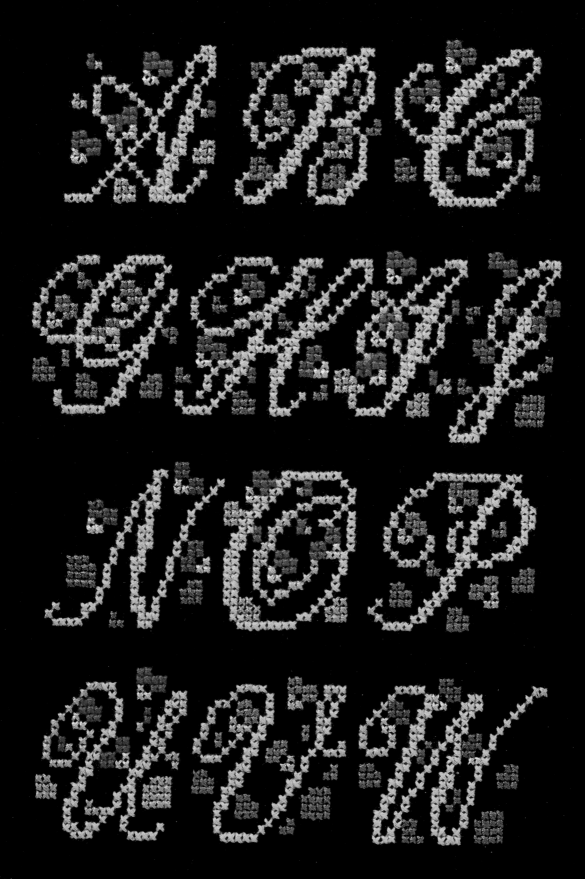

Instructions on page 94.

Instructions on page 57.

9

10

Instructions on page 58.

12

Instructions on page 60.

Instructions on page 61.

13

SMALL ITEMS

Instructions on page 62.

ABCDEF
GHIJKL
MNOPQ
RSTUV
WXYZab
cdefghijklmno
pqrstuvwxyz

Instructions on page 96.

Holbein stitch with 3 strands (792)

Use six strands of DMC #25 six-strand embroidery floss unless otherwise indicated.

⊡ = 776	△ = 445	● = 601	⊕ = 956	◎ = 603
▽ = 740	⊥ = 742	▼ = 741		
‖ = 799	Ս = 209	○ = White	Ζ = 792	▲ = 501
⊠ = 912	⧄ = 913			

Use four strands of DMC #25 six-strand embroidery floss.

◖=814	**#**=816	**■**=304	**=**=891	**⊠**=783	**O**=726	**⊘**=3078	**◖**=746	**H**=501
L=502	**S**=503	**●**=326	**◉**=309	**λ**=335	**∅**=956	**E**=957	**/**=899	**↓**=3326
•=776	**□**=819	**☑**=818	**⊕**=3347	**▲**=936	**C**=368	**〈**=704	**V**=987	**◢**=300
◉=349	**%**=350	**F**=351	**⊖**=352	**⊘**=743	**T**=937	**U**=470	**◇**=471	**Z**=734
▲=740	**☊**=741	**I**=742	**◤**=745	**◆**=434	**◮**=832	**⚠**=3013		

50

Holbein stitch with
3 strands (920)

(911)

Use four strands of DMC #25 six-strand embroidery floss.

▲ = 740	Ω = 741	I = 742	O = 726	T = 937	◆ = 471	U = 470	▲ = 704	II = 976
◎ = 604	△ = 605	+ = White	L = 830	∩ = 911	S = 989	− = 913	● = 326	⊖ = 309
⋋ = 335	• = 776	☑ = 818	▼ = 829	V = 987	◆ = 920	⊗ = 922	✕ = 307	⊢ = 3689
✕ = 972	⊥ = 973	∧ = 733	# = 730	■ = 550	⋋ = 552	⊘ = 553	▽ = 554	⟨ = 209
I = 991	⁒ = 992	∕ = 943	⬿ = 3346	∅ = 956	⊤ = 986			

Use three strands of DMC #25 six-strand embroidery floss.

| $\boxed{V}$ = White | $\boxed{X}$ = 3041 | $\boxed{/}$ = 3042 | $\boxed{\blacktriangle}$ = 552 | $\boxed{/\!\!/}$ = 553 | $\boxed{\odot}$ = 210 | $\boxed{\|}$ = 550 | $\boxed{\ominus}$ = 814 |
| $\boxed{\cap}$ = 602 | $\boxed{\cdot}$ = 961 | $\boxed{\blacklozenge}$ = 938 | $\boxed{\square}$ = 818 | $\boxed{O}$ = 3689 | $\boxed{+}$ = 209 | $\boxed{\varnothing}$ = 211 |

Use three strands of DMC #25 six-strand embroidery floss.

☑ = White ■ = Black ● = 327 ⋒ = 602 ⊘ = 553 ◉ = 210
☒ = 3041 △ = 554 ○ = 3689

Shown on page 6

Use five strands of DMC #25 six-strand embroidery floss.

⊡ = 349 ⊕ = 350 ◎ = 351 ▽ = 754 I = 760 Z = 608 L = 740 / = 704 X = 906

V = 907 ▲ = 890 ▼ = 905 D = 470 T = 830 ø = 833 π = 666 + = 893 ◉ = 326

△ = 727 ◬ = 742 ◐ = 407 ⊖ = 976 ● = 645

Use five strands of DMC #25 six-strand embroidery floss.

⊙ = 819	• = 3689	⊕ = 605	◎ = 603	◉ = 602	☐ = White	◢ = 814	⬘ = 730
⤢ = 992	◢ = 704	⊟ = 3348	‖ = 554	⊗ = 718	▽ = 552	● = 550	▽ = 472
⟋ = 704	▽ = 725	⊺ = 210	⊕ = 211	⩔ = 209	⊘ = 833	△ = 742
⅄ = 745	⊠ = 906	⩔ = 209	✚ = 208	△ = 973	

Use four strands of DMC #25 six-strand embroidery floss.

◎ = 3051 Ⅱ = 732 ✕ = 701 ⚟ = 602 − = 907 □ = 947 ⊗ = 792 ◇ = 793
⅄ = 725 ⌀ = 971 ◤ = 910 ◒ = 798 △ = 943 ● = 600 ∨ = 993 • = 996

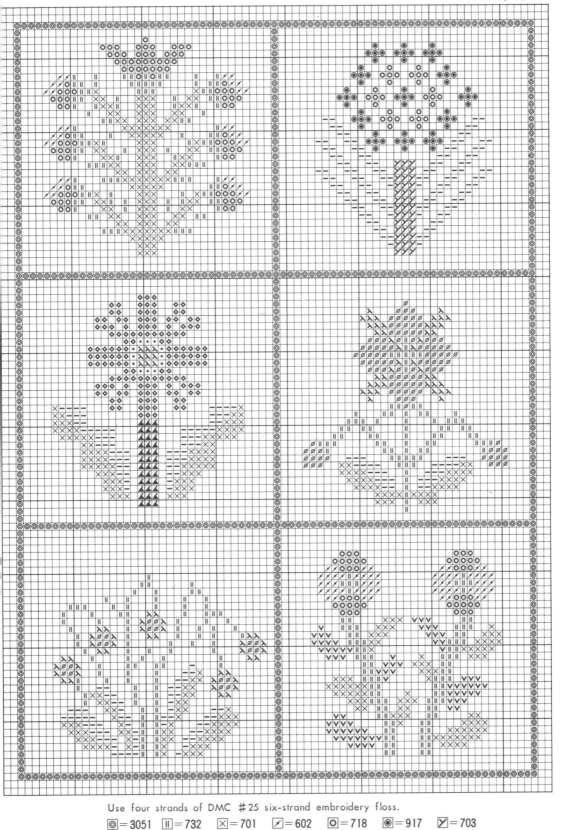

Use four strands of DMC #25 six-strand embroidery floss.

◎ = 3051   ‖ = 732   ☒ = 701   ⁄ = 602   Ⓞ = 718   ◉ = 917   Ⓨ = 703

— = 907   ◈ = 793   • = 996   ⅄ = 725   ◣ = 910   ∅ = 971   Ⓥ = 993

Shown on page 10

Use four strands of DMC #25 six-strand embroidery floss.

Symbol	Color	Symbol	Color	Symbol	Color	Symbol	Color	Symbol	Color
☑ =	701	⊟ =	703	⊠ =	907	◎ =	956	◢ =	904
⊞ =	905	⊡ =	973	◙ =	700	⊗ =	3345		
● =	824	⊠ =	943	∅ =	742	△ =	996	⊥ =	906
⊠ =	326	◉ =	807	⟋ =	3347				

Use four strands of DMC #25 six-strand embroidery floss.

⊗ = 3345　‖ = 905　✕ = 907　● = 915　◎ = 603　○ = 605　◢ = 433　◐ = 435

╱ = 3347　△ = 702　▲ = 937　◉ = 741　∅ = 742　T = 743　□ = 3078

Use four strands of DMC #25 six-strand embroidery floss.

☒ = 725   ⊙ = 833

Straight stitch with
2 strands (725)

Use four strands of DMC #25 six-strand embroidery floss.

☒ = 725   ◎ = 833

Use three strands of DMC #25 six-strand embroidery floss.

Ⲧ = 783	● = 817	Y = 435	◆ = 904	∅ = 3326	‖ = 601	X = 699	✕ = 989	◢ = 400
+ = White	< = 743	O = 760	✳ = 806	L = 988	◢ = 552	♎ = 554	◉ = 600	T = 841
∥ = 519	⦶ = 796	# = 816	Λ = 745					

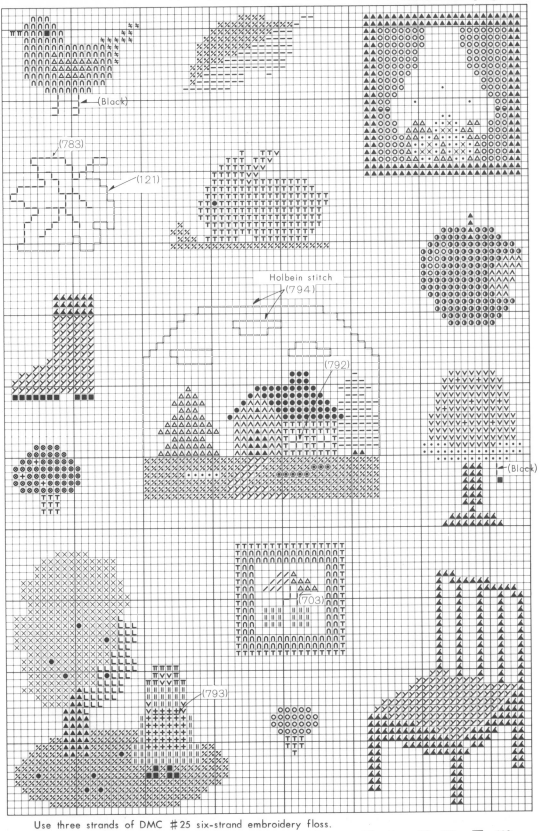

Use three strands of DMC #25 six-strand embroidery floss.

⋂ = 794	⋇ = 806	⊓ = 783	▣ = Black	⊠ = 989	⊟ = 986	▲ = 801	Ⓞ = 760	⊙ = 600
⊠ = 725	• = 209	△ = 701	T = 841	V = 776	◉ = 304	∧ = 745	+ = White	◣ = 400
⦿ = 817	◎ = 962	⊿ = 435	⊗ = 335	⊠ = 699	L = 988	‖ = 601	∕ = 703	

Use two strands of DMC #25 six-strand embroidery floss.

Ⓞ = White	△ = 800	✗ = 943
◎ = 606	⧄ = 471	S = 3347
✶ = 3345	⊠ = 208	Z = 892
◗ = 992	• = 311	⋋ = 703
L = 931	C = 210	D = 742

◿ = 993	T = 435	▽ = 957	Ⅰ = 947	● = 336	▲ = 799
▼ = 414	‖ = 434	+ = 209	╤ = 501	◖ = 601	⊥ = 603
⊡ = 307	◮ = 666	⦿ = 996	V = 602	▢ = 754	✳ = 995
⟋ = 312	⊗ = 798	◨ = 946	◓ = 762	▲ = 930
◉ = 701	⚊ = 970			

Holbein stitch (435)(892)

(892)

(943)

Holbein stitch
(312)

(931)

(312)

(995)

Use two strands of DMC #25 six-strand embroidery floss.

C = 210	● = 336	L = 931	F = 437	T = 435	◉ = 606	◖ = 601	+ = 209	△ = 666
Z = 892	I = 947	▲ = 800	▽ = 957	■ = 301	− = 956	Ω = 718	X = 943	⁒ = 552
⊥ = 603	✳ = 995	◐ = 996	◨ = 307	S = 3347	‖ = 434	◎ = 701	λ = 703	⊤ = 501
✕ = 500	v = 602	◣ = 992	⁄ = 993	O = White	▼ = 414	✶ = 3345	⦸ = 3348	□ = 754
◤ = 796	✸ = 900	⋂ = 415	⟨ = 445	⦰ = 598				

Holbein stitch with
2 strands (917)

Use three strands of DMC #25 six-strand embroidery floss unless otherwise indicated.

◢ = 820	◉ = 311	▲ = 975	∨ = 452	◓ = 3021	⊕ = 350	✕ = 304	∪ = 905
◑ = 814	▢ = 809	∅ = 972	Φ = 781	♎ = 3064	L = 211	• = 352	▽ = 727
△ = 955	● = 838	◎ = 798	⊢ = 917	◆ = 433			

Straight stitch
with 2 strands.
(986) (3345)

Use three strands of DMC #25 six-strand embroidery floss unless otherwise indicated.

O = 828	◉ = 920	◢ = 934	• = 352	⁄ = 943	∩ = 993	⊗ = 912	L = 977	◐ = 781
△ = 726	⁄ = 676	∅ = 972	U = 905	● = 801	◢ = 300	⅍ = 841	T = 3051	I = 988
▽ = 986	◉ = 601	▲ = 369	✕ = 937	V = 3346	F = 581	λ = 470	◑ = 904	Z = 816
C = 891	π = 336	S = 327	✕ = 915	E = 701	⁄ = 907	△ = 909	⊢ = 580	✳ = 731
D = 831	— = 783	Ω = 729	▽ = 738	‖ = 3045	＜ = 962	✳ = 733	▼ = 3345	⊥ = 704
+ = 472	◎ = 434	╤ = 612	✶ = 437					

< 90 >

Straight stitch
(807)

Use two strands of DMC #25 six-strand embroidery floss.

$\boxed{-}$ = 554 $\boxed{⊼}$ = 807 $\boxed{■}$ = 915 $\boxed{◎}$ = 603 $\boxed{▲}$ = 600 $\boxed{S}$ = 319 $\boxed{Y}$ = 988 $\boxed{⅀}$ = 830

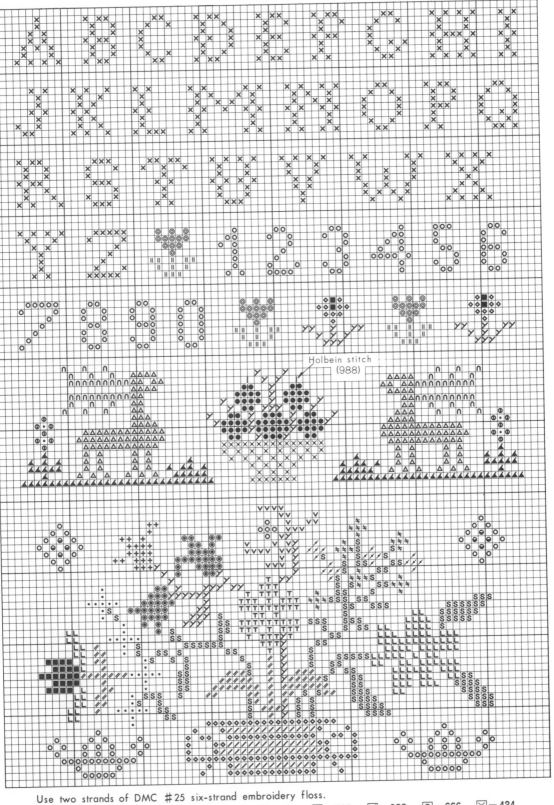

Holbein stitch
(988)

Use two strands of DMC #25 six-strand embroidery floss.

☒ = 912	◎ = 603	Ⅱ = 895	○ = 725	■ = 915	◈ = 798	⅄ = 988	● = 666	⊠ = 434
△ = 632	⋂ = 611	⏀ = 553	• = 444	◢ = 986	⬒ = 740	◉ = 550	+ = 208	⊔ = 718
T = 335	V = 604	⁄ = 806	✳ = 807	S = 319	⟋ = 3346	⁄ = 813		

Straight
stitch (890)

Use two strands of DMC #25 six-strand embroidery floss.

☒ = 718	⊙ = 604	⊘ = 209	◉ = 321	⊞ = 828	⊡ = 818
⊡ = 988	⊻ = 353	◎ = 898	■ = Black	◁ = 414	Ⲧ = 783

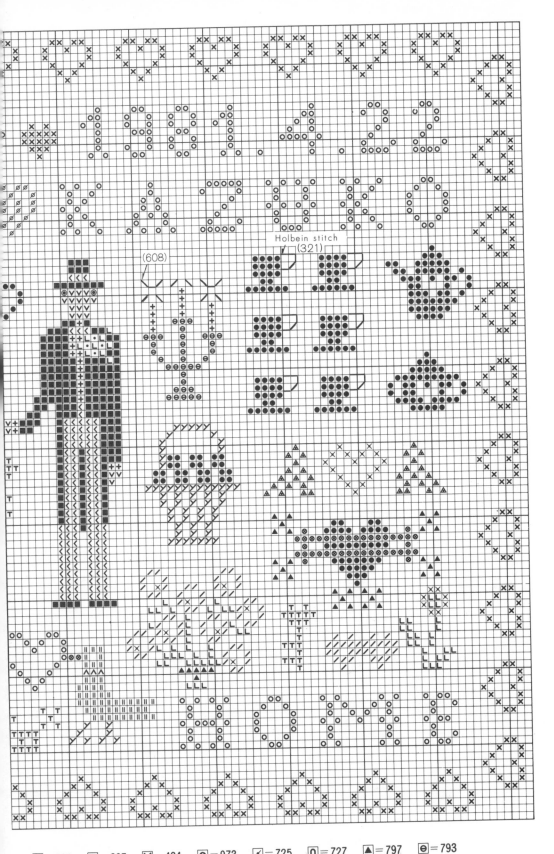

Holbein stitch
(321)

(608)

II = 806 Λ = 807 Y = 434 ⊗ = 973 ∕ = 725 ∩ = 727 ▲ = 797 ⊖ = 793

⊢ = 839 ◢ = 904 λ = 3346 H = 890 X = 915 ∕ = 603 △ = 993

Use two strands of
DMC #25 six-strand
embroidery floss.

X = 783	▲ = 3345	▲ = 3346	△ = 3347	X = 552	∅ = 553	╱ = 554
◉ = 601	⊛ = 602	O = 603	■ = 991	▲ = 413	⊖ = 317	Y = 414
I = 415	T = 943	Z = 917	◆ = 915	Φ = 970	• = 971	∩ = 957

Holbein stitch (823)

Use three strands of DMC #25 six-strand embroidery floss.

$\boxed{O}$ = White	$\boxed{\circledcirc}$ = Ecru	$\boxed{\oplus}$ = 646	$\boxed{\bullet}$ = 844	$\boxed{/}$ = 740	$\boxed{\triangledown}$ = 742	$\boxed{\blacktriangle}$ = 351	$\boxed{\blacktriangledown}$ = 350

$\boxed{X}$ = 801 $\boxed{\%}$ = 3041 $\boxed{/}$ = 349 $\boxed{V}$ = 319 $\boxed{\boxtimes}$ = 894 $\boxed{+}$ = 762 $\boxed{T}$ = 415 $\boxed{I}$ = 745

$\boxed{\cdot}$ = 783 $\boxed{\vdash}$ = 725 $\boxed{}$ = Black (Holbein stitch)

Use three strands of DMC #25 six-strand embroidery floss.

• =	907
◹ =	470
⊤ =	730
▽ =	937
✕ =	992
▽ =	367
◢ =	500
O =	648
N =	640
⊖ =	646
◎ =	645
+ =	839
⟩ =	433
⫽ =	221
✕ =	312
◁ =	793
⊕ =	794
☐ =	211
⫽ =	931
⊃ =	932
⊥ =	831
⌀ =	680
╱ =	676
I =	729
◣ =	677
⊥ =	224
● =	Black Holbein stitch
☐ =	Black

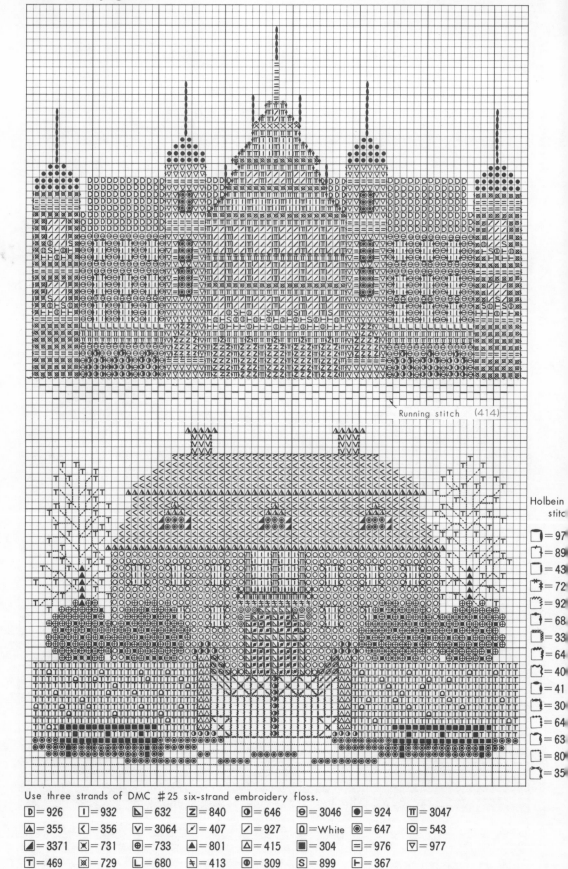

Running stitch (414)

Holbein
stitc

☐ = 97
☐ = 89
☐ = 43
☐ = 72
☐ = 92
☐ = 68
☐ = 33
☐ = 64
☐ = 40
☐ = 41
☐ = 30
☐ = 64
☐ = 63
☐ = 80
☐ = 35

Use three strands of DMC #25 six-strand embroidery floss.

D = 926	I = 932	◣ = 632	Z = 840	◐ = 646	⊖ = 3046	● = 924	π = 3047	
▲ = 355	◁ = 356	∨ = 3064	◿ = 407	╱ = 927	◨ = White	◎ = 647	O = 543	
◪ = 3371	✕ = 731	⊕ = 733	▲ = 801	△ = 415	■ = 304	= = 976	▽ = 977	
T = 469	⊠ = 729	L = 680	⊰ = 413	◉ = 309	S = 899	⊢ = 367		

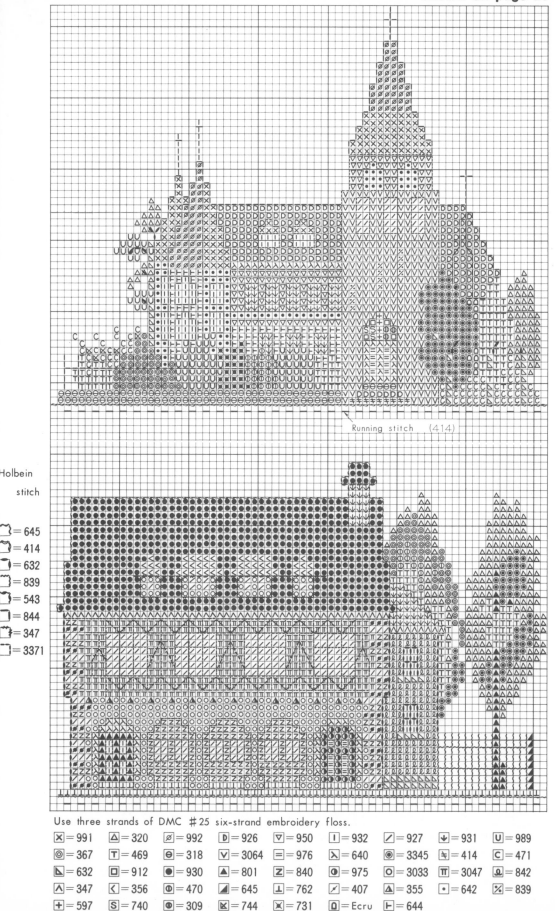

Running stitch (414)

Holbein
stitch

⊃ = 645
⊃ = 414
⊃ = 632
⊃ = 839
⊃ = 543
⊃ = 844
⊃ = 347
⊃ = 3371

Use three strands of DMC #25 six-strand embroidery floss.

⊠ = 991	△ = 320	⦰ = 992	Ð = 926	▽ = 950	Ɩ = 932	╱ = 927	⬇ = 931	Ʊ = 989
◎ = 367	⊤ = 469	⊖ = 318	⊽ = 3064	═ = 976	λ = 640	◉ = 3345	⚹ = 414	C = 471
◣ = 632	☐ = 912	● = 930	▲ = 801	Z = 840	◐ = 975	O = 3033	π = 3047	Ω = 842
⋀ = 347	⟨ = 356	Φ = 470	◢ = 645	⊥ = 762	╱ = 407	△ = 355	• = 642	⅍ = 839
✚ = 597	S = 740	Φ = 309	⊠ = 744	⊠ = 731	▯ = Ecru	⊢ = 644		

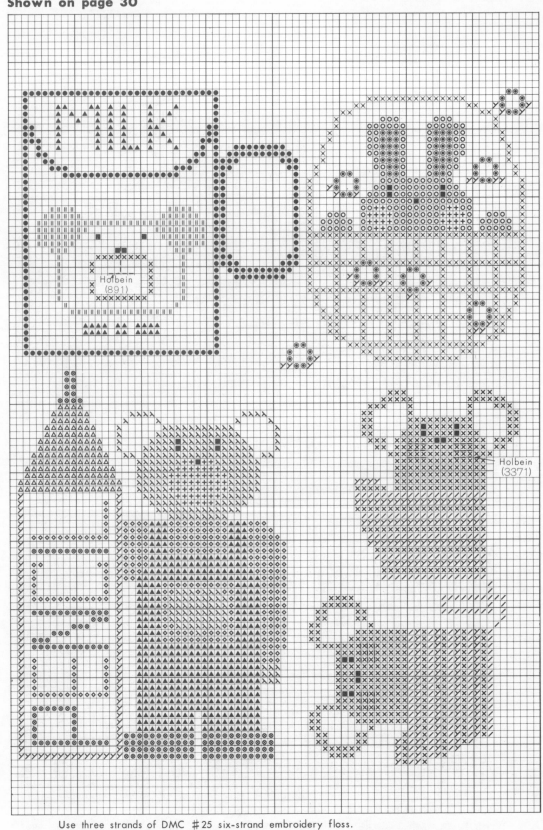

Use three strands of DMC #25 six-strand embroidery floss.

●=891 ▲=312 ■=3371 ‖=742 ☒=744 ☒=3064 ◉=956 ○=963

☒=988 ✚=White ✲=718 ◈=554 △=Ecru λ=3325 ╱=3348

Holbein stitch
(3371)

Use three strands of DMC #25 six-strand embroidery floss.

$\boxtimes$ = 744 $\triangle$ = Ecru $\diagup$ = 3348 $\circledcirc$ = 956 $\bigcirc$ = 963 $\blacksquare$ = 3371 $\boxplus$ = White $\boxed{Y}$ = 988

$\boxed{\bullet}$ = 891 λ = 3325 $\blacktriangle$ = 312 $\|$ = 742 $\diamondsuit$ = 554 $\otimes$ = 718 $\boxtimes$ = 3064

Shown on page 32

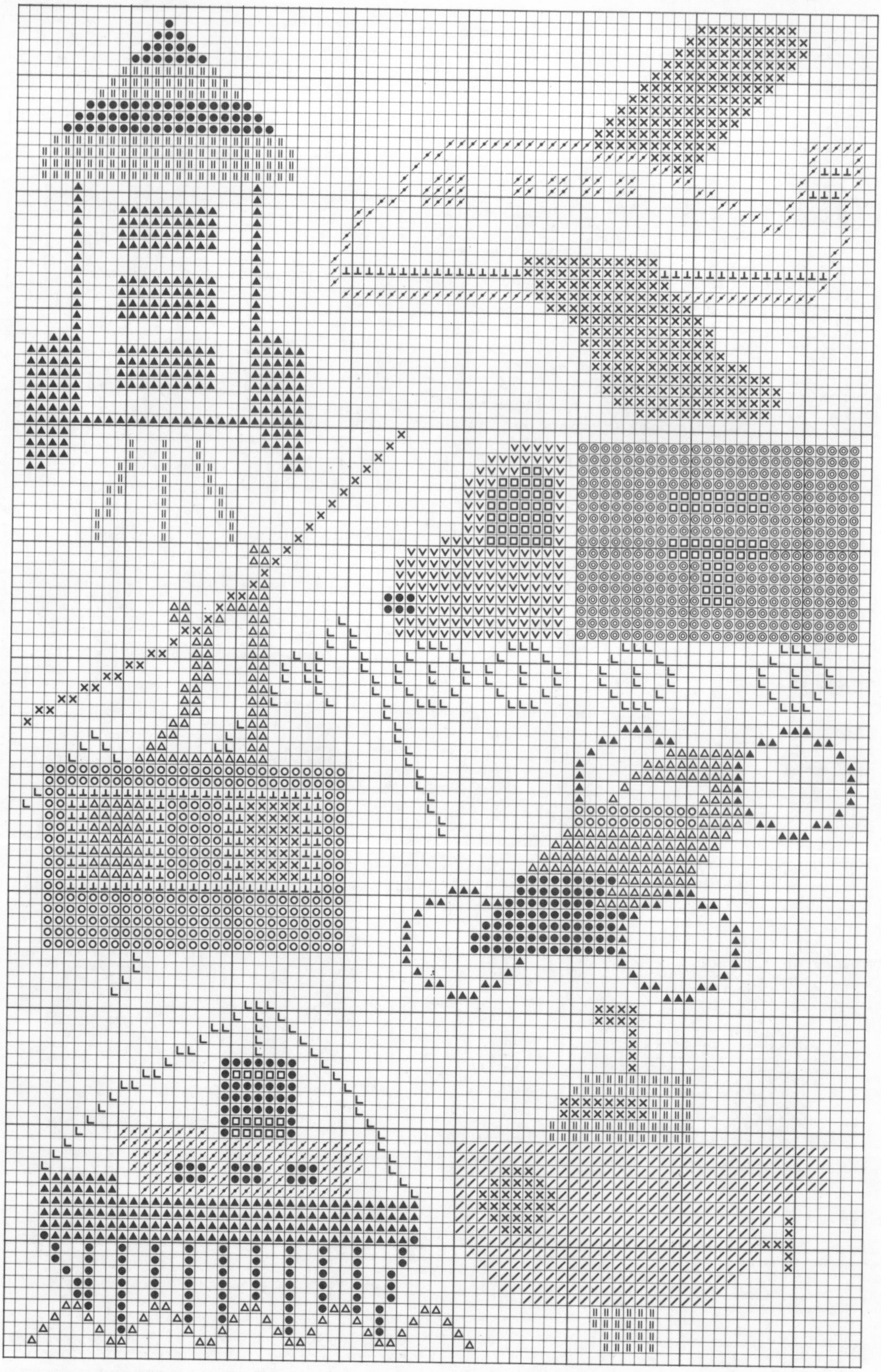

Use three strands of DMC #25 six-strand embroidery floss.

●=321 ‖=972 ▲=824 ⁄=911 ⊥=744 ×=704 △=799 ○=894

L=975 ◎=350 V=422 □=White /=718

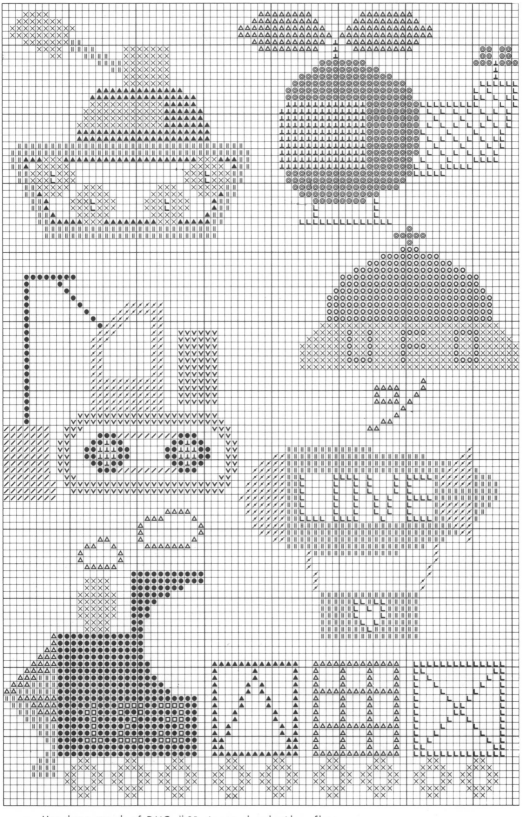

Use three strands of DMC #25 six-strand embroidery floss.

$\boxtimes$ = 704 $\boxed{\text{II}}$ = 972 $\blacktriangle$ = 824 $\boxed{\text{L}}$ = 975 $\triangle$ = 799 $\circledcirc$ = 350 $\perp$ = 744 $\bullet$ = 321

$\diagup$ = 911 $\boxed{\text{V}}$ = 422 $\diagup$ = 718 $\bigcirc$ = 894 $\boxed{\square}$ = White

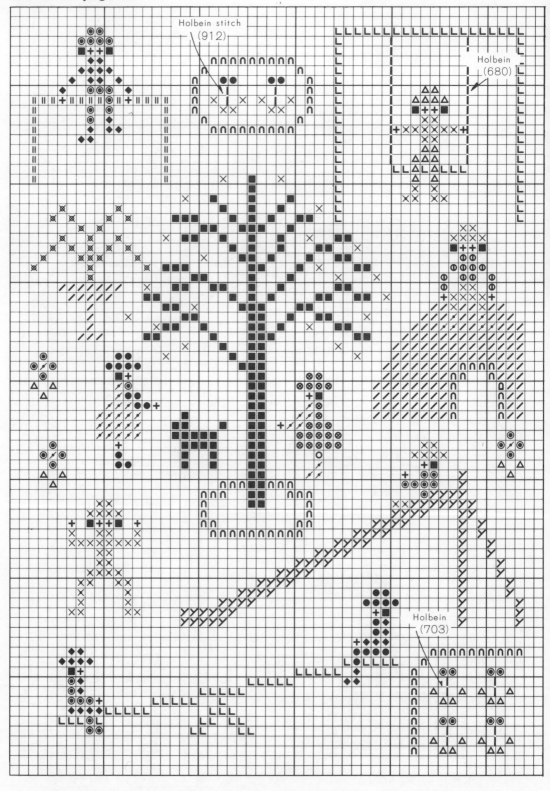

Use six strands of DMC #25 six-strand embroidery floss.

‖ = 834	+ = 754	◉ = 602	◆ = 792	■ = 610	∩ = 3032	● = 608	⊠ = 912	L = 680
☒ = 793	△ = 703	▨ = 807	╱ = White	⊗ = 604	⟋ = 742	Φ = 740	Ɏ = 733	

Use six strands of DMC #25 six-strand embroidery floss.

⊗ = 604   ◐ = 601   ⁄ = 742   ◆ = 792   ⊖ = 605   ➕ = 754   ∩ = 3032   ● = 608

⊠ = 807   ✕ = 912   △ = 703   ■ = 610   ╱ = White   ⦶ = 740

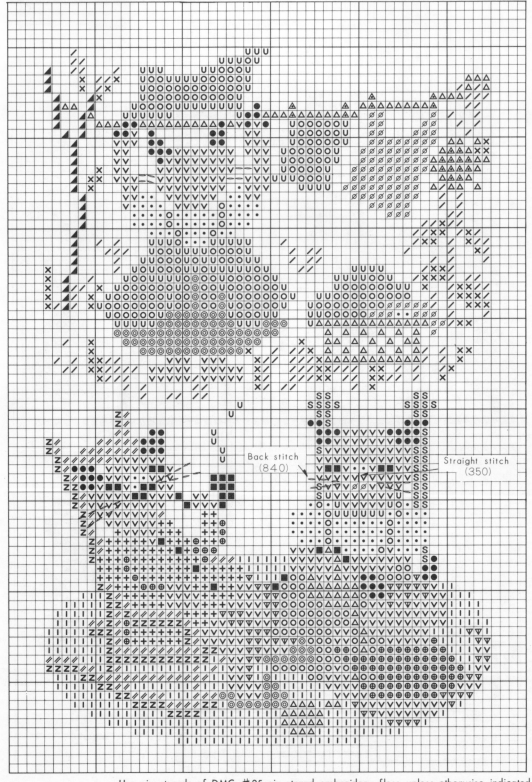

Use six strands of DMC #25 six-strand embroidery floss unless otherwise indicated.

O = White	**U** = 794	**△** = 973	**▲** = 971	**◢** = 632	**●** = 840	**V** = 436
• = 604	**∅** = 350	**◎** = 602	**■** = Black	**╱** = 704	**X** = 906	**⊕** = 553
+ = 209	**▽** = 435	**I** = 605	**Z** = 912	**╱** = 954	**S** = 798

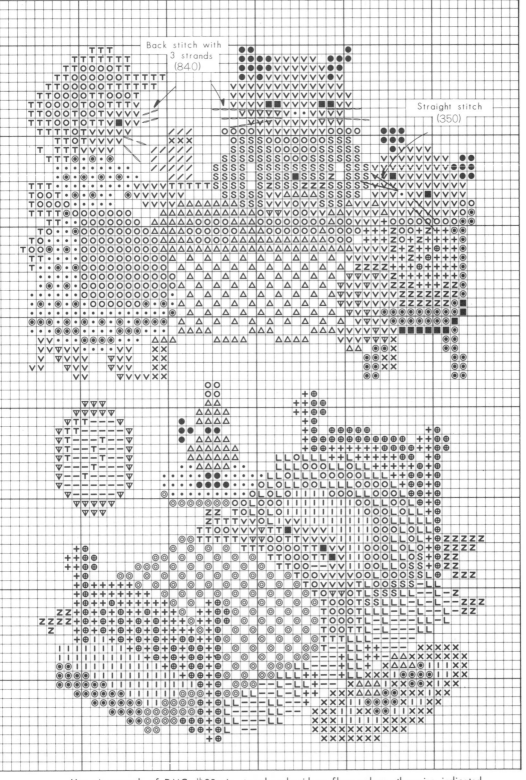

Back stitch with
3 strands
(840)

Straight stitch
(350)

Use six strands of DMC #25 six-strand embroidery floss unless otherwise indicated.

O = White   ● = 840   ▽ = 435   V = 436   T = 598   • = 604   ∕ = 913

△ = 743   X = 992   Z = 792   ■ = Black   + = 210   ⊕ = 208   S = 793

L = 813   − = 775   ◎ = 602   ◉ = 351   I = 776

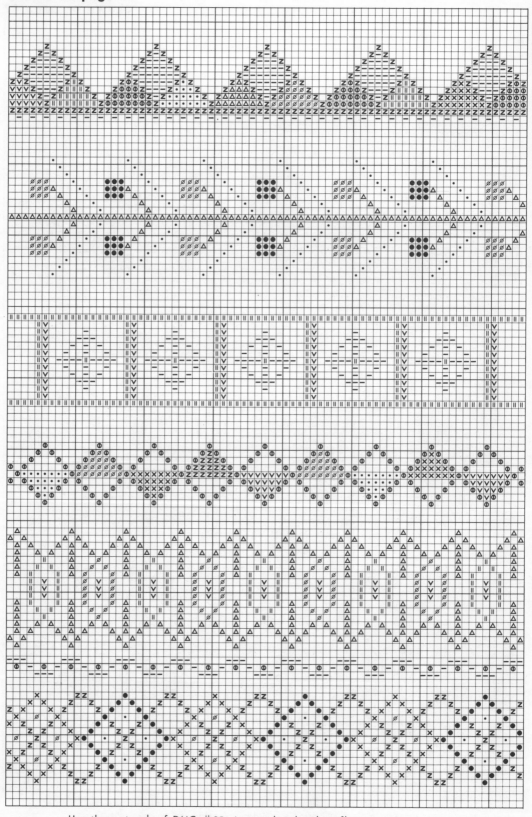

Use three strands of DMC #25 six-strand embroidery floss.

Z = 3022   — = 893   V = 472   II = 208   Φ = 996   • = 703

△ = 700   ø = 972   ● = 326   X = 797

Use three strands of DMC #25 six-strand embroidery floss.

◢ = 995 ◎ = 970 • = 703 ‖ = 208 ∅ = 972 ✗ = 797

● = 326 ⊠ = 704 △ = 700 ⦿ = 996

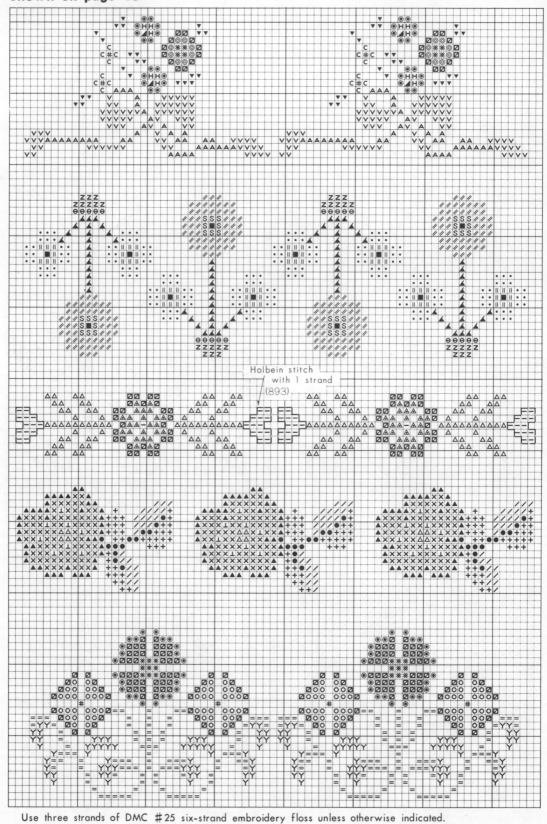

Holbein stitch
with 1 strand
(893)

Use three strands of DMC #25 six-strand embroidery floss unless otherwise indicated.

V = 210	A = 208	◢ = 498	H = 3326	◎ = 3350	☑ = 893	▼ = 334	C = 813	⬕ = 798
S = 791	⊖ = 920	Z = 922	◣ = 3011	• = 807	‖ = 995	■ = 445	− = White	◭ = 608
▲ = 946	X = 741	△ = 704	⊥ = 731	● = 831	∕ = 3348	+ = 470	= = 320	Y = 368
◉ = 335	O = 894	# = 742	✳ = 725					

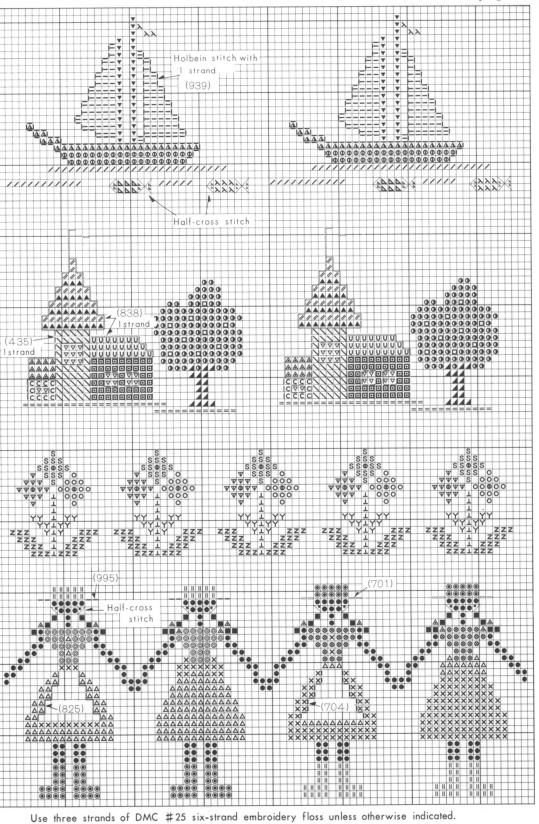

Holbein stitch with
1 strand
(939)

Half-cross stitch

(838)
1 strand

(435)
1 strand

Half-cross
stitch

(995)

(701)

(825)

(704)

Use three strands of DMC #25 six-strand embroidery floss unless otherwise indicated.

⧄ = 747	◣ = 553	⋋ = 899	◉ = 912	◮ = 806	▼ = 939	▤ = 320	▽ = 828	▲ = 815
⧄ = 321	◢ = 838	▢ = 972	U = 806	▣ = 738	◥ = 3047	C = 951	◐ = 3346	⊥ = 731
■ = 844	Z = 502	Y = 368	S = 917	▼ = 600	O = 602	◉ = 907	X = 825	● = 801
△ = 704	‖ = 995	◮ = 608	◎ = 444	⊗ = 956	◉ = 701	- = White		

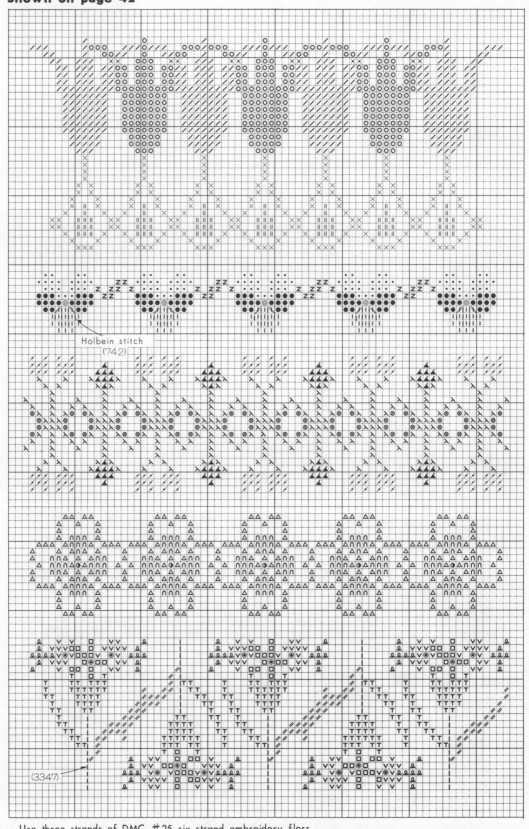

Holbein stitch
(742)

(3347)

Use three strands of DMC #25 six-strand embroidery floss.

◢ = 807	◯ = 912	☒ = 992	☒ = 704	⫿⫿ = 725	● = 550	• = 208	Ⅰ = 210	Z = 988
◎ = 742	◿ = 961	◣ = 963	⊗ = 469	⅄ = 471	△ = 741	∩ = 351	◖ = 839	▢ = 826
∨ = 807	♌ = 799	◉ = 726	T = 3347	⫽ = 3346

Holbein stitch
(913)

Use three strands of DMC #25 six-strand embroidery floss.

◢ = 3350   ⊖ = 961   ⚹ = 3688   ✚ = 3326   ⅄ = 3053   Ⓢ = 3011   = = 3013

⟁ = 740   ⟨ = 742   ⌀ = 726   ▽ = 729   Ⓤ = 470   ⅄ = 471   ∧ = 519

⟋ = 807   Ⓛ = 813   ▲ = 208   ◆ = 304   ✕ = 992

Holbein stitch
(930)

(838)

Use three strands of DMC #25 six-strand embroidery floss.

⦿ = 315   ‖ = 316   Ⓞ = 778   ✖ = 930   ▲ = 838   ╱ = 840

Holbein stitch (221)

Holbein stitch (3011)

Holbein stitch (3021)

Use three strands of DMC #25 six-strand embroidery floss.

⊙ = 3021   + = 3328   ∨ = 3011   ⊕ = 347   △ = 3013   T = 782   ◇ = 677   ▲ = 632   ⁄ = 221

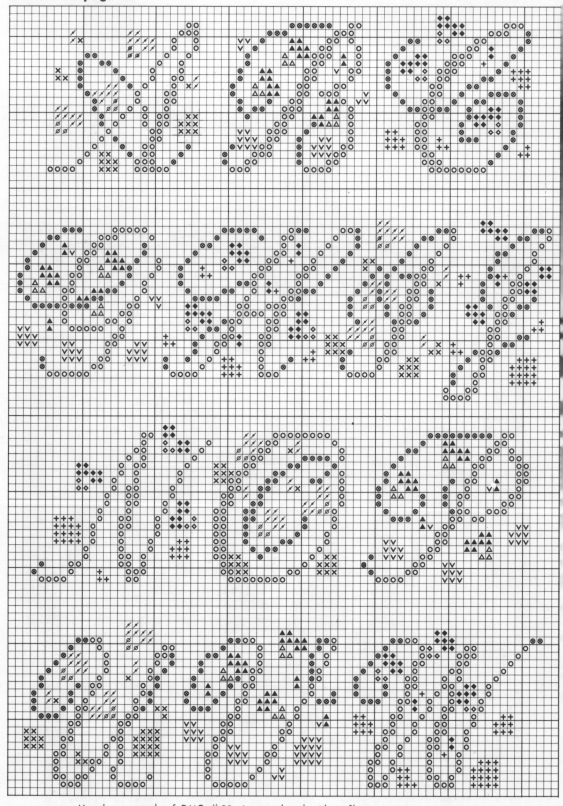

Use three strands of DMC #25 six-strand embroidery floss.

⊗ = 725   Ⓞ = 973   ⟋ = 917   ⊘ = 3689   ☒ = 598   ▲ = 799   △ = 800

☑ = 911   ◆ = 552   ◈ = 211   ⊞ = 470

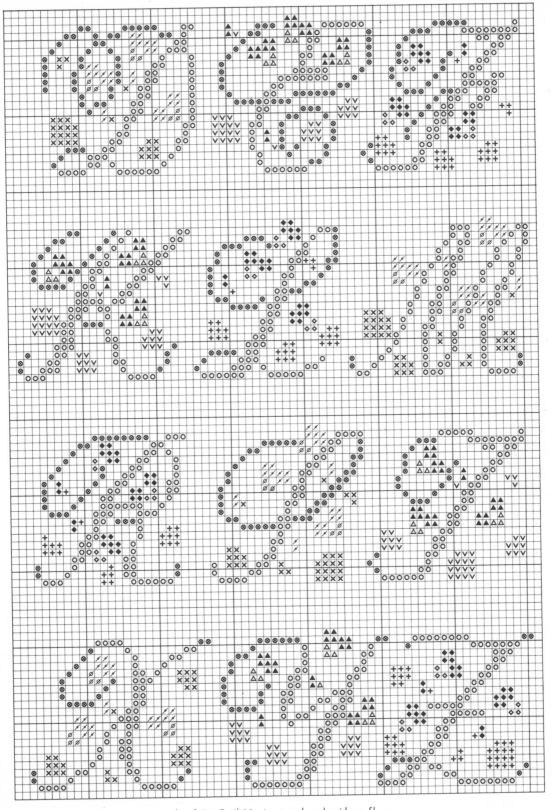

Use three strands of DMC #25 six-strand embroidery floss.

⊗ = 725   ◎ = 973   ⁄ = 917   ∅ = 3689   ⊠ = 598   ▲ = 799   △ = 800

∨ = 911   ◆ = 552   ◇ = 211   ✛ = 470

L-68 D-46
R-48 T-28

Use three strands of DMC #25 six-strand embroidery floss.

$\boxed{\times}$ = 498 $\boxed{\odot}$ = 312 $\boxed{/}$ = 781 $\boxed{\triangle}$ = 319 $\boxed{+}$ = 351 $\boxed{O}$ = 469 $\boxed{\vee}$ = 799

$\boxed{\diamond}$ = 869 $\boxed{\lambda}$ = 598 $\boxed{\cdot}$ = 915

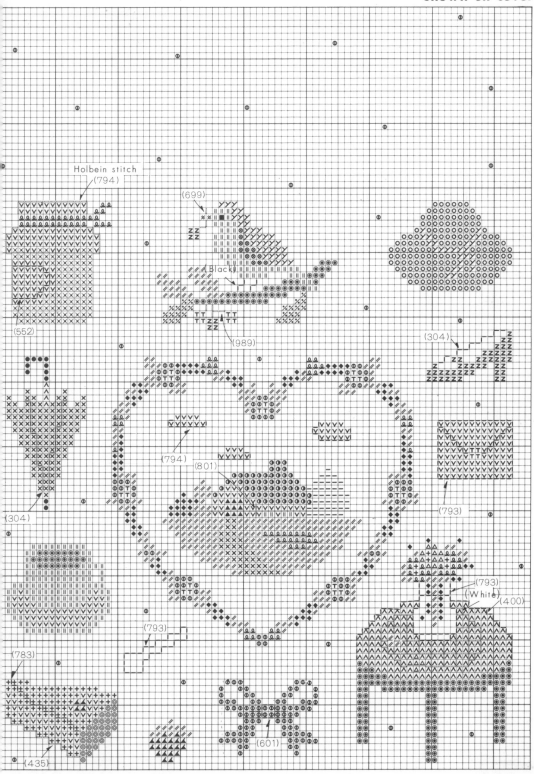

Holbein stitch
(794)

(699)

(Black)

(552)

(989)

(304)

(794)

(801)

(793)

(304)

(793)

(793)

(793)

(White)

(400)

(783)

(601)

(435)

Use three strands of DMC #25 six-strand embroidery floss.

▼ = White	◉ = 817	▲ = 801	✕ = 760	Ω = 209	‖ = 794	Φ = 3326	T = 601	◆ = 986
∅ = 989	✕ = 600	● = 796	◉ = 400	◎ = 435	▲ = 304	✕ = 783	Y = 792	⊗ = 806
■ = Black	✕ = 699	Z = 304	− = 987	O = 725	∧ = 841	△ = 962	+ = 745

Let's learn Basics in
Cross Stitch for a neater finish.

Cross Stitch

In Cross Stitch, the design is worked regularly by making crosses in the same direction. Use the even-weave fabrics or canvas which you can count the threads easily. You may use a checked fabric like gingham as a guide for Cross Stitch. Use a blunt needle made for Cross Stitch with which you can pick up the threads easily. You may use a blunt tapestry needle when working on heavy-weight fabrics, wool or knit.

To work horizontally:

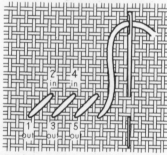

Work across all stitches in each row from left to right.

When coming to the end, cross back in the other direction from right to left.

To work downward horizontally:

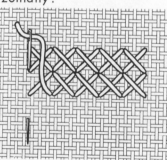

To work upward horizontally:

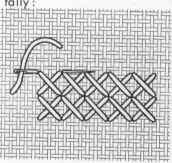

To Complete each cross horizontally:

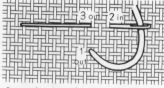

Bring the thread out at the lower left and take a stitch from 2 to 3.

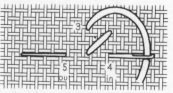

Insert the needle at 4 and take a stitch to 5.

Continue to work, completing each cross.

To complete each cross vertically:

Bring the thread out at the upper right and take a stitch from 2 to 3.

Insert the needle at 4 to form a cross and take a stitch to 5.

Take a stitch from 6 to 7.

Complete each cross working vertically. The direction of the threads must be the same, when working downward or upward.

To work upward diagonally:

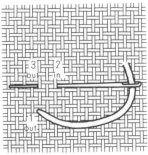 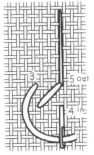  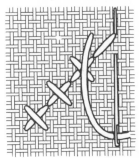

Bring the thread out at 1 and take a horizontal stitch from 2 to 3.

Take a vertical stitch from 4 to 5.

Continue to work upward diagonally, completing each cross.

To work downward diagonally:

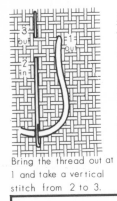 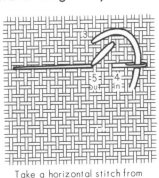 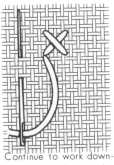 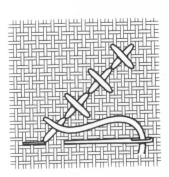

Bring the thread out at 1 and take a vertical stitch from 2 to 3.

Take a horizontal stitch from 4 to 5.

Continue to work downward diagonally, completing each cross.

Overcast the cut-edge before you work.

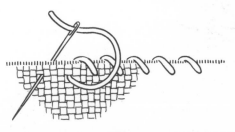

Suitable fabrics for Cross Stitch are easy to fray. Overcast the cut-edge before you start working for easy handling.

Holbein Stitch

This is also called Line Stitch and is sometimes used for outlining or dividing cross-stitched area. The stitch is completed by running stitches in both ways. Stitches on the wrong side are the same on the front.

Straight Line:

Take stitches of equal length.

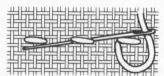

When coming to the end of design, return in the same way filling in the spaces left by the first row. Always insert the needle in the same direction for a neater finish.

Diagonal Line:

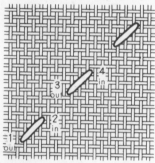

Take stitches of equal length diagonally.

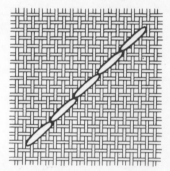

When coming to the end of design, return in the same way as for the Straight Line.

Zigzag Line

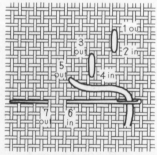

Take vertical stitches from upper right.

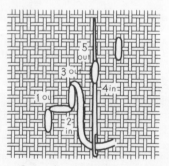

Bring the thread at 1 and take a vertical stitch from 2 to 3.

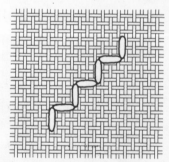

On return journey, take horizontal stitches to make zigzag line.

Half Cross Stitch

Usually only half of the cross is made for Half Cross Stitch, but in this book we use the stitch as shown on the right.